ANCIENT CIVILIZATIONS

ANCIENT
ROME

BY SUSAN E. HAMEN

Essential Library

An Imprint of Abdo Publishing | www.abdopublishing.com

ANCIENT
ROME

BY SUSAN E. HAMEN

CONTENT CONSULTANT

Thomas Keith, Lecturer
Department of Classical Studies
Loyola University Chicago

www.abdopublishing.com

Published by Abdo Publishing, a division of ABDO, PO Box 398166, Minneapolis, Minnesota 55439.
Copyright © 2015 by Abdo Consulting Group, Inc. International copyrights reserved in all countries.
No part of this book may be reproduced in any form without written permission from the publisher.
Essential Library™ is a trademark and logo of Abdo Publishing.

Printed in the United States of America, North Mankato, Minnesota

102014
012015

Cover Photos: Vladimir Korostyshevskiy/Shutterstock Images, foreground; iStock/
Thinkstock, background

Interior Photos: iStock/Thinkstock, 3, 10; Shutterstock Images, 6–7, 37, 45, 55, 89 (left); Lebrecht
Music and Arts Photo Library/Alamy, 14–15; DIZ Muenchen GmbH, Sueddeutsche Zeitung Photo/
Alamy, 19; Hoberman Collection/Corbis, 21; Asier Villafranca/Shutterstock Images, 23; Alfredo Cerra/
Shutterstock Images, 25; S. Borisov/Shutterstock Images, 28–29; Dorling Kindersley/Thinkstock, 31,
51, 85; North Wind Picture Archives/Alamy, 36; Marco Cristofori/Alamy, 38–39; Red Line Editorial, 46,
77; iStockphoto, 52–53, 61, 62–63, 80–81; Reinhard Dirscherl/Alamy, 54; Antony McAulay/Shutterstock
Images, 69; Chad Matthew Carlson/Shutterstock Images, 70–71; Marco Secchi/Alamy, 79; Jeffrey B.
Banke/Shutterstock Images, 89 (right); Viacheslav Lopatin/Shutterstock Images, 90–91, 97; Daniel M.
Silva/Shutterstock Images, 95

Editor: Rebecca Rowell
Series Designer: Jake Nordby

Library of Congress Control Number: 2014943874

Cataloging-in-Publication Data

Hamen, Susan E.
 Ancient Rome / Susan E. Hamen.
  p. cm. -- (Ancient civilizations)
ISBN 978-1-62403-542-5 (lib. bdg.)
Includes bibliographical references and index.
1. Rome--Civilization--Juvenile literature. 2. Rome--History--Juvenile literature. 3. Rome--Social life
and customs--Juvenile literature. I. Title.
937--dc23

                              2014943874

CONTENTS

CHAPTER 1

A MIGHTY EMPIRE

In March 44 BCE, a young Roman man named Octavian learned his great uncle, the mighty Gaius Julius Caesar, had been murdered. Caesar had been a general in the Roman army before becoming a statesman, an authority figure in Roman politics, and then head of the government. Along the way, Caesar had made enemies.

The Pantheon has survived the centuries to become a popular tourist attraction.

BETRAYAL AND ASSASSINATION

The ruling body of Rome, the Senate, did not care for the tactics Caesar used to gain political power with his allies Crassus and Pompey. After the death of Pompey in 48 BCE, Caesar became the most powerful man in Rome. Some senators feared he would use his power to crown himself king. They plotted to assassinate Caesar. His murder prompted a series of civil wars within Rome. The Roman Republic started unraveling.

The Assassination of Julius Caesar

The assassination of Julius Caesar has become legendary, inspiring playwright William Shakespeare to recount the man's life and death in the play *Julius Caesar*. On the Ides of March (March 15 according to the Roman calendar) in 44 BCE, Caesar made his way to the Theatre of Pompey for a meeting of the Senate. There, conspirators confronted him, including Tillius Cimber, who presented Caesar with a petition to allow his exiled brother to return to Rome. When Caesar declined, Cimber grabbed him. Another conspirator, Casca, attacked Caesar with a sharpened writing instrument called a stylus. Immediately, all the men with Cimber began attacking and stabbing Caesar. Brutus, a Roman politician and Caesar's friend, was among them, which prompted Shakespeare's famous line uttered by the dying Caesar, "*Et tu, Brute?*" which is Latin for "You too, Brutus?"[1]

With 23 stab wounds, Caesar bled to death on the Senate floor. The assassins marched to the city's capitol, rejoicing and announcing that the city was once again free. The citizens of Rome, however, remained in their homes and did not join in the revelry. The assassination of Caesar brought about years of civil war and unrest.

In his will, Caesar adopted Octavian and made the 19-year-old his sole heir. The young man took the name Gaius Julius Caesar Octavianus. He then began an ascent to power that would usher in a new era in Rome.

Caesar's chief lieutenant, Mark Antony, took control of Rome after Caesar's murder. Octavian raised an army of men who had been loyal to the assassinated Caesar, and they defeated Mark Antony in 43 BCE. Octavian forced the Roman Senate to elect him to a high-ranking position. He then struck an agreement with Mark Antony, and the two men, along with an ally of Caesar named Lepidus, divided the existing provinces among themselves. Mark Antony took control of Rome's eastern provinces. Octavian ruled the western provinces. Lepidus oversaw Rome's territory in North Africa.

The next year, in 42 BCE, Octavian joined military forces with Mark Antony, and the two defeated Caesar's assassins. Octavian had avenged the death of Caesar and had risen to formidable power within Rome.

THE AGE OF THE ROMAN EMPEROR

Octavian did not settle for sharing the rule of Rome. In 32 BCE, he went to war against Mark Antony. The two had earlier removed Lepidus from power, leaving only the two of them in control of Rome. In the Battle of Actium on September 2, 31 BCE, Octavian's general, Marcus Agrippa, defeated the armies of Mark Antony and his lover, Queen Cleopatra of Egypt. Antony and Cleopatra killed themselves, leaving Octavian to become Rome's sole leader.

In 27 BCE, the Senate gave Octavian the name Augustus, which means "revered one."[2] Initially, he directed Rome's civil and military affairs. With time, he gained more and more power. He divided the city of Rome into administrative areas and granted the business class, the *equites*, influence in decisions about how the city should be run.

Rome thrived under Augustus's rule. The empire doubled in size as Rome's armies advanced into Europe. Augustus also expanded Rome's highway system throughout the empire. After years of battles and civil

ANCIENT ROME AT ITS GREATEST SIZE (117 CE)

ROME

N

unrest, he brought a lasting peace to the Roman Empire and set out to restore the city of Rome itself. He had monuments and buildings repaired, bridges and aqueducts constructed, and marble brought from the north to turn Rome from a city of brick into a city of gleaming white marble. He established Rome's first police force and fire department. He kept the people of Rome content with grain and money.

Augustus ushered in the era of the Roman Empire. His patience and diplomacy made him a great leader, and the Roman citizens believed the gods favored Augustus. His rule became known as the Age of Augustus. During this time, trade, art, and literature flourished.

Augustus died of old age in 14 CE, marking a 41-year reign. The Romans made him a god and worshiped him for his many accomplishments. The Roman Empire Augustus helped establish would endure for centuries.

MODERN AND MEMORABLE

Ancient Rome was the first modern city. At its peak, the empire spanned three continents, covering 2 million square miles (5 million sq km) and ruling more than 60 million people.[3] Rome was the first civilization to unite the Western world under its rule. Rome was more than the city on the west coast of the Italian Peninsula. The empire stretched west into Britain, north into

Germany, and south into North Africa, including Egypt. Rome became known as *Caput Mundi*, "the Head of the World."[4]

Rome's engineering and architectural marvels, many of which remain today, are evidence of the advanced intelligence and skill of the Romans. For example, between 70 and 80 CE, the Romans built the Colosseum in the city of Rome from concrete and stone using simple hand tools. The arena could hold 50,000 to 80,000 spectators.

Writers crafted enduring works of literature and poetry that scholars today still consider important. Examples include Virgil's epic poem *Aeneid*

Rome's Geographic Benefits

The location of the city of Rome was paramount to the empire's success. Rome's geographical position allowed for protection, sea access, freshwater, and suitable land.

The Apennine Mountains extended across the southeast of Rome and stretched north, protecting it from invaders coming from Europe. The steep banks of the Tiber River, upon which Rome was built, also provided protection against invaders.

In addition, the Tiber flowed into the Mediterranean Sea, providing Rome with an excellent port that allowed for trade with Greeks, Africans, and other seafaring peoples. And the Mediterranean climate of hot, dry summers and wet, mild winters allowed people, plants, and animals to thrive. The rich volcanic soil was ideal for farming.

and Ovid's poem *Metamorphoses*. Latin, the language spoken in Rome and throughout much of the Roman Empire, was the precursor to the Romance languages, including Italian, Spanish, and French.

The wealth and success of Rome came from the lands and peoples it conquered. Rome's military prowess was unparalleled at the time. Its might made fighting off the advance of Roman soldiers virtually impossible for any foreign land. The Romans enjoyed the spoils of war, including natural resources such as gold and marble, which they seized for the emperor.

As Rome continued its rise in power, evidence of military conquests arose throughout the city. Statues, columns, and buildings carved from gleaming white marble announced Rome's greatness throughout the Empire.

Roman law and politics have served as the basis upon which several civilizations and countries have designed their political systems. For example, the Roman code of law helped form the basis for codes of law in Europe, including the Napoleonic Code, a civil code of law in France that was established under Napoléon Bonaparte in 1804.

The age of ancient Rome changed the world. Its architecture, art, literature, engineering feats, military conquests, and system of government helped shape people and places near and far and left a legacy as the world's first superpower.

CHAPTER 2

HUMBLE BEGINNINGS

Scholars know little history of the area that would become the city of Rome prior to the 700s BCE. Historians agree that Rome's story begins with a very ancient city called Alba Longa. It was located a short distance southeast of Rome. Alba Longa was the most powerful city in that region, called Latium, beginning in approximately the 1100s BCE. Historians

An Etruscan stone coffin shows the artistic skill of these people who settled Latium.

widely accept that Alba Longa was the center of the league made up of approximately 30 Latin cities in the area and had some sort of rule over them.

The history of Alba Longa is mixed with so much myth that historians have difficulty obtaining a true historical knowledge of the area. Alba Longa did function as a kingdom from approximately 1150 BCE to the mid-700s BCE, when Rome was founded. A century after Rome began, its king, Tullus Hostilius, destroyed Alba Longa in war, sparing only its temples.

EARLY ROME

Limited knowledge exists about the true history of Rome from the time of Alba Longa to the founding of the city of Rome. Archaeologists do know the mighty metropolis began as a humble settlement of farmers and shepherds. In the early 700s BCE, present-day Italy was populated with multiple tribes, including the Etruscans and the Latins.

In approximately 1000 BCE, small village communities along the Tiber River united into a single settlement of agricultural people. They called their new settlement Rome. A small group of huts in an area known as Palatine Hill was Rome's nucleus.

The river offered freshwater and transportation, both of which helped Rome develop. By the 700s and 600s BCE, the Romans had cleared woods and drained swamps to expand their farmland. The settlement had evolved into an important city-state that was growing in size and sophistication.

By 600 BCE, the Etruscans, who were the most advanced civilization in northern Italy, took control of the city of Rome. The town continued to prosper as the Etruscans cultivated trade and commerce and built roads and public buildings. A series of seven Etruscan kings ruled the growing city until 509 BCE. During their reign, in approximately 575 BCE, the Romans leveled two marshy areas to make way for a cattle market and the Roman Forum, a marketplace. Roman citizens fell into two classes. Patricians were property-owning noblemen from wealthy families. Plebeians were common, working-class people who depended upon the patricians. Slaves, who were not considered citizens, also lived in the city.

Although Rome was thriving, the people were displeased with their Etruscan king, a harsh ruler named Lucius Tarquinius Superbus. Roman nobles overthrew him in 509 BCE and set out to establish

Founding Myth

Early Romans turned to a myth for answers to Rome's history. Legend states that twin sons of the god of war, Mars, founded Rome on April 21, 753 BCE. According to the legend, Romulus and Remus were the grandsons of Numitor, king of Alba Longa. His daughter was the twins' mother. Numitor's brother, Amulius, left the infant twins to drown in the Tiber River when he overthrew the king. The infants, in a basket, washed ashore. A female wolf found and fed them. A shepherd's family raised the twins, who were later reunited with their grandfather. They grew up and founded a city. An argument over who should rule it resulted in Romulus killing Remus. Romulus then became Rome's first king, naming the city in honor of himself.

a new form of government that would allow Rome to transition from a monarchy to a republic, or *res publica*, which is Latin for "property of the people."

THE RISE OF THE ROMAN REPUBLIC

By the time the Etruscan royal family was banished, Rome had grown into a walled city. A series of wars and victories over neighboring settlements left Rome the most powerful city-state in central Italy.

As Rome prospered, Romans were eager for a government that allowed the people more power. The early years of the republic brought about a ruling body called the Senate. It consisted of elected officials called senators, who served different levels of office and decided how Rome should be organized and run. They also passed laws and controlled the army. Initially, only patricians could serve as senators, leaving the working class with no control. By 367 BCE, plebeians could hold the office of consulship, the highest office in Rome.

EXPANSION

By the 200s BCE, Rome had gained control of the Italian Peninsula. Then, during the First Punic War (264–241 BCE), the Romans took the island of Sicily from Carthage, a trading center and sea power on the northern coast

An artist imagines Hannibal's army fighting the Romans with elephants during the Second Punic War.

of Africa (modern-day Tunisia). Countries or regions taken under control by Rome were called provinces. Sicily became Rome's first province.

Rome battled Carthage again during the Second Punic War (218–201 BCE). Hannibal, a mighty Carthaginian general, attacked Rome from the north when he brought his army, complete with 6,000 horses and a few elephants, through the Alps into Italy.[1] The Romans defeated Hannibal's army in 202 BCE. The victory gave Rome the Carthaginian provinces in Spain.

During the Third Punic War (149–146 BCE), Rome destroyed the city of Carthage and annexed portions of northern Africa and more of Spain.

In 146 BCE, Rome expanded into Greece and Macedonia and soon gained portions of land in modern-day Turkey.

Rome's conquests brought great wealth. The Romans took the spoils of war, such as marble and gold. They also brought slaves back to Rome to work the land of upper-class citizens and their expanding holdings. Slaves were important resources. Free men could be drafted into military service, but slaves were exempt. That meant landowners might lose their paid laborers to military service but not slave labor.

Appian, a Greek historian and Roman citizen, explained that during this time "powerful citizens became immensely wealthy and the slave class all over the country multiplied," while common laborers suffered under "poverty, taxes, and military service."[2] Peasant landowners were forced to give up their small, less productive farms as the aristocrats' *latifundia*, large expanses of land used to produce profitable crops, continued growing. These huge farms did not offer employment to the displaced smaller farmers because slaves worked the land without wages. Rome's poor population grew as the social structure degraded. The result was a civil war.

INTERNAL CONFLICT

In 133 BCE, the government official Tiberius Sempronius Gracchus attempted to enforce landholding limitation laws that had been established in the

200s BCE but not enforced. A group of senators murdered him. Because senators were from the wealthy upper class that continued to get richer, they did not favor reform that would transfer any kind of power or wealth to the working class. Although he had made a fervent attempt to help those less fortunate, Gracchus was unsuccessful in acquiring reform for poorer citizens.

Rome also suffered slave revolts and an invasion by Germanic tribes. Rome had to arm the poor to avoid complete defeat. The door opened for powerful military generals to seize control. In 60 BCE, Pompey, Crassus, and Julius Caesar formed a pact called the First Triumvirate. The trio grew powerful within the Senate. However, when Crassus was killed in battle, Pompey and Caesar turned on

Julius Caesar, who was immortalized on Roman coins, rose to power during a time of turbulence yet prosperity.

one another. Caesar eventually defeated Pompey and his loyal supporters and took control of Rome for himself. He declared himself dictator for life in 45 BCE and was the sole ruler of the Roman world. The following year, on March 15, 44 BCE, a group of senators killed Caesar, fearing he was becoming an emperor. His death marked the end of the Roman Republic.

THE RISE OF THE ROMAN EMPIRE

After defeating Mark Antony and gaining Egypt for Rome in 31 BCE, Octavian, Caesar's grand-nephew and adopted son, became Rome's first emperor, soon taking the name Augustus. This marked the beginning of the Roman Empire. Augustus was the first of many emperors who would control the strongest empire on earth. Some emperors were wise and good, supporting public works projects and improving life within the city of Rome. Other emperors were cruel, power-hungry tyrants.

Rome reached the height of its power from 96 to 180 CE. Emperor Claudius pushed troops as far as Britain in 43 CE and into North Africa (modern-day Morocco and Algeria), further expanding the empire. Trajan, who ruled from 98 to 117 CE, brought the empire to the peak of its expansion, pushing into Dacia (modern-day Romania and Hungary), as well as parts of the Middle East (modern-day Jordan, Saudi Arabia, and Iraq). Rome had become a superpower, governing more than 60 million people across three continents.[3]

The Romans erected towns and cities as far away as Wales and Scotland as Roman armies took control in those areas. Great wealth poured into Rome in the form of gold and silver cups, plates, and other items the Romans had taken from conquered lands and melted to create Roman money. Trade and commerce across the empire thrived. The Romans created buildings, statues, and monuments using marble, stone, gold, and other precious materials from faraway lands. Opulence and luxury abounded for the wealthy.

Rome's first emperor, Augustus, stands tall and strong in this marble statue uncovered at Prima Porta, near Rome.

A CLOSER LOOK

POMPEII

In 79 CE, Vesuvius erupted and destroyed Pompeii and Herculaneum, located near the Bay of Naples. Signs of an impending eruption were present, including an earthquake. But Pompeii's population was caught completely unaware.

On the morning of August 24, the eruption started. Ash and pumice fell first. By midnight, hot ash, pumice, rock fragments, and volcanic gas rushed down the side of the mountain. Fumes coming from Vesuvius were toxic, making breathing deadly. Refugees fled to the harbor, but there was no time to evacuate them. Pompeii was completely covered in successive blankets of black ash and pumice. One-tenth of the population—2,000 Pompeians—died in the blast. Many of them died almost instantly.[4]

The eruption left behind an incredible record of Roman life that was undiscovered for centuries. The ash encased Pompeians and created hardened molds around their bodies. The bodies disintegrated, but the molds remained. By carefully injecting plaster into the molds, archaeologists were able to recreate detailed forms of the victims, capturing their expressions of pain and agony. Vesuvius had preserved Pompeii as though it had been frozen in time.

Eventually, archaeologists unearthed much of the city, excavating entire houses and public buildings, along with streets and artifacts. Researchers found beautiful fresco paintings on house walls and discovered pottery, jewelry, and other household items. By studying the remains of Pompeii, historians were able to learn much about everyday life in an ancient Roman city.

Languages of the Empire

Although Latin is considered the language of ancient Rome, Greek was also a dominant language. Latin was the language of the courts and the military, and many traders and businessmen used it. As the empire expanded, the Romans conquered peoples who did not speak Latin. The empire expected such groups to acquire at least a rudimentary understanding of the language.

Educated upper-class citizens studied and were fluent in Greek. They used this language for diplomatic communications with their Greek neighbors. When the West Roman Empire dissolved, Greek became the dominant language in the East Roman Empire, later known as the Byzantine Empire.

THE SPLIT

Rome's vastness eventually contributed to its downfall. The empire became too large for one man to control effectively. Roman armies in distant lands became more loyal to their commanding officers than to their emperor. Rome battled enemies in Europe and Asia, and rivals fought to claim the title of emperor.

In 284 CE, Diocletian became emperor. He reorganized the Roman government, dividing it into smaller provinces to create stability. He also standardized Roman coins and attempted to implement price controls. His efforts would not endure.

In 395, Arcadius and Honorius, the sons of Emperor Theodosius I, split the Roman Empire in two: the West Roman Empire and the East Roman Empire. Rome remained the capital in the West. Constantinople became the capital in the East.

In the early 400s, Germanic tribes began invading and looting cities under Roman control in Spain and Africa. In 410, the Visigoths, a Germanic group, sacked the city of Rome. Meanwhile, formerly conquered groups such as the Celts and Saxons fought Roman occupation. And in 455, Gaiseric, a Vandal leader, led his people in an attack on Rome. They plundered the mighty city. In 476, Odoacer, a Germanic leader, knocked Romulus Augustulus from power. The West Roman Empire had fallen.

The East Roman Empire remained intact for nearly another 1,000 years. It thrived as the Byzantine Empire. In 1453, the Ottomans took control of Constantinople and made it the capital of their empire. After enduring for more than 20 centuries, the rule of Rome had come to an end.

CHAPTER 3

THE GOVERNMENT AND ECONOMY

When the Roman Republic overthrew the king and took power in 509 BCE, a new system of government began. Instead of one monarch ruling Rome, the Senate became the most powerful governing body.

Ruins of the Temple of Saturn, *left*, and the Temple of Castor and Pollux, *right*, still stand in the Roman Forum.

The Senate had 300 to 600 senators.[1] The number fluctuated over time. Senators, always men, were former magistrates, or government officials. In order to become a senator, a man first had to serve as a military officer. The next step was to be elected as a quaestor, or financial official. Once a man was elected quaestor, the lowest position in the Senate, he became part of the Senate for life, unless the other senators expelled him. The next position was aedile, or a public works official. He could then hold a higher office within the Senate: the position of praetor, or judicial official.

These positions could not be held one right after the other. Magistrates would hold each office for one year, after which they would return to their private lives for one year. Each year, two consuls were elected to head the government and command the army in times of war. Because these positions were unpaid, only the wealthy could afford to serve as consuls.

Initially, only patricians could serve in government. By the 300s and 200s BCE, plebeians gained a degree of power after serving in the military to help fight wars. They banded together and formed their own assembly, the *Concilium Plebis*. They did not have power over the Senate, but they did confirm magistrates to their position within the Senate. The assembly also provided a discussion forum in which the people could voice their concerns.

GOVERNMENT STRUCTURE
OF THE ROMAN REPUBLIC, 80 BCE

Patricians

Senate (300+ members)
Managed foreign policy and controlled policy. Proposed but could not pass laws; advised the consuls.

Consuls (2)
Managed the army and the government. Each could veto the other. Generally served a one-year term.

- In emergencies, one consul could become a dictator for six months.
- After leaving office, could become a censor; censors conducted a census of Rome every five years.

Praetors (8)
Judges; also administered the law. Could become a provincial governor after leaving office.

Aediles (16)
In charge of specific aspects of government, such as buildings, food supply, or games.

Quaestors (20)
Managed government finances and administration.

Tribunes (10)
Represented the plebians.

Ordinary People
Townsfolk, farmers, soldiers, freed slaves

Slaves
Considered possessions with no rights. Included farm workers, mine workers, gladiators, and servants.

Soldier and Slave

Plebeians

The assembly elected its own leaders, called tribunes, who fought for causes in the working class. In 287 BCE, plebians succeeded in winning the right to have decrees they passed carry the force of law. Finally, in matters of politics and religion, they were equal with the patricians. The tribunes had the power to veto any law the Senate made. Still, the real control of power remained with the richest families serving in the Senate.

THE AGE OF EMPERORS

When members of the Senate killed Caesar in 44 BCE, they did so to keep the republic functioning as the government of Rome. While they succeeded in killing Caesar, they failed in achieving their goal. After a civil war, Octavian brought peace to Rome. He became the first emperor of the Roman Empire in 27 BCE and took the name Augustus. After nearly 500 years of functioning as a republic, Rome had one ruler.

Augustus's rise to power ushered in a new form of government. The Senate continued and retained some power, but the emperor could overrule its decisions. The emperor had supreme authority, including control of the army, the ability to create new laws, and the authority to nominate consuls. He relied on personal advisers to help him make laws and head the army.

The emperor also chose senators and consuls. Elections continued, but the emperor nominated the candidates, ensuring his preferred people would be elected. The Senate lost a considerable amount of power.

LAWS AND THE LEGAL SYSTEM

Rome's legal system developed with the city, republic, and empire. In 451 BCE, the Roman Republic published *Lex XII Tabularum*, "Law of the Twelve Tables," which was the empire's first code of law. Ten commissioners wrote it for the sake of plebeians, who believed court decisions were made from unwritten laws based on custom and were known only to a small group of patricians. The Twelve Tables did not establish new laws. Rather, the group put existing laws in writing that could be read and understood by everyone. The plebeians believed laws should be established and set in writing for all to know, so they could protect themselves against patricians abusing their power. All Romans respected the Twelve Tables as a prime source of legal rules. With time, the code became more complex, and

Paternal Law

The Twelve Tables, published in 451 BCE, set forth a variety of rules, including guidelines for trials, inheritance and guardianship, public law, and sacred law. This was the first official collection of Roman laws that all citizens used. Many laws addressed the rights of fathers, with one entire table dedicated to the power of the paterfamilias, or male head of the household, over his family. The Twelve Tables granted him the authority to decide if a child in the family lived or died. The Twelve Tables also alluded to Rome's dependence upon farming and producing crops. It included punishments for causing another person to lose the use of a limb, which interfered with his or her ability to farm.

ancient Rome became the first Western society to have professional lawyers. Citizens also elected judges.

Over time, a set of legal principles called the *ius gentium*, "law of nations," arose. It took a more common sense approach to the law and focused on fairness, as opposed to the *ius civile*, "citizen law," laws that were specific to the political community of Rome. In 438 CE, a group of legal experts working under the orders of Emperor Theodosius II created the Theodosian Code. This and the *Digest*, a collection of law cases and decisions that Emperor Justinian collected in the 500s CE, provide much of what is now understood about the system of Roman law.

TRADE

The Roman Empire provided a common market for a vast area of land and millions of people. Most people living in the western portions of the empire could speak Latin, which facilitated commerce. Traders moved goods by sea and on roadways. Regular shipping trade routes crossed the sea between Rome and Egypt. Imports aplenty came into the city of Rome from around the world.

With an ever-growing population, the city of Rome had a substantial need for food. Each year, Rome imported more than 400,000 short tons (300,000 metric tons) of grain from Africa, Egypt, and Sicily.[2] Spain provided a variety of goods, including black wool, honey, olive oil, red dye, wax, and wine. France supplied wine, while Syria provided glassware and cloth. Greece was a source for clothing items, such as shoes. Merchant ships also brought precious natural resources from beyond the empire's borders: marble from North Africa and Asia, silks from the Far East, and gemstones from India. Rome was a bustling, thriving metropolis.

Currency

During the early republic, Romans did not use coins. They used bronze weights until the 300s BCE. These were odd lumps of bronze that could be weighed on a scale. Value of the bronze was based on how much it weighed—greater weight meant greater value. Eventually, oblong bricks of bronze began to circulate.

The Romans began using coins in approximately 280 BCE. Their first coins were silver. Later, the Romans made coins from metals brought from other lands, including gold, silver, and bronze.

Coins guaranteed a widely recognized value and made trade easier. Roman coins also spread the image of the current ruler because the emperor's profile was typically minted onto the currency. The silver denarius became the principal coin of Rome until the 200s CE. Troops ensured these coins experienced wide circulation throughout the Roman Empire. Cities, especially in the East, continued minting local coins, though Roman coinage was accepted throughout the empire.

A CLOSER LOOK

THE ROMAN FORUM

The Roman Forum began as a cattle market in Rome's early days. It was situated at the center of the city. Over time, it became a central meeting place. Markets continued in the Forum, which was simply an open space. It also became the center of civic life. Street vendors mingled with magistrates in the bustling locale.

The courts of law, the Senate House, and offices of the city's important businessmen and bankers were arranged around the Forum. Temples also occupied space in the Forum's perimeter. Every day, senators met in the Forum. Over time, the place grew to be quite crowded. Pieces of the Forum's various structures remain today.

CHAPTER 4

DAILY LIFE

People living in ancient Rome fell into one of several categories. These categories included full citizens; various levels of partial citizens without the right to vote; noncitizens; slaves; and freedmen. Most of the population consisted of noncitizens. As Rome spread, more people were given the privilege of citizenship. Women and children could hold the status of citizenship, but they were not allowed to vote.

Romans enjoyed baths far from their homeland, including in England.

Male Roman citizens could own property, vote, and serve in the army as a legionnaire or an officer, and they were protected by Roman law. Women had fewer privileges than men. As time passed, Roman women were granted the right to own property and conduct business in their own name if they gave birth to at least three legitimate children. However, they were not allowed to vote and could not hold public office.

Slaves were considered property and not entitled to any of the rights or protections of Roman law. Masters had the right to beat or kill any slave for any reason. Some masters treated slaves cruelly, but not all masters did so. Rather, many masters endeavored to take care of their investment. Sometimes, slaves became like a member of the master's family. A master could grant a slave freedom. It was common for a master to free slaves for performing exemplary service or to leave instructions that slaves be freed upon his death. These slaves were known as freedmen. They became Roman citizens and were free to participate in Roman society, but they could not hold political office. And if a former owner was still alive, a freed slave owed him a certain number of service days per year.

Parking Problems

The size of the city of Rome led to enormous traffic problems. Because of the multitude of people, carts were not allowed on city streets except at night. Large parking areas, called *areae carruces*, complete with paid parking attendants, provided a place for carts and other vehicles during the day.

Slaves played an important role in Rome's success. They provided free labor, which allowed wealthy patricians to profit from their large farming villas. For most of the empire's existence, Rome had access to a seemingly endless supply of slaves. Conquered lands provided more land area and resources for Rome, including people who could be taken into slavery. Rome's army sent many people from defeated lands to Rome to serve as farm laborers and house workers. The Romans forced slaves to work in mines and to build a variety of structures, including bridges, roads, and monuments.

PATERFAMILIAS

The oldest living male was the head of the Roman household. The paterfamilias, literally "father of the family," had absolute power over his family. He ran the family's business affairs and owned the family's property. His sons could not own property until he died, regardless of their age. Adult sons with their own families had no way of making their own money until their father died. They also had no legal power over their own children until his death. Instead, they relied upon the paterfamilias for a *peculium*, or allowance.

Families valued boys, wanting sons to carry on the family line. Many still loved and welcomed daughters. However, some families mourned the birth of a daughter. The paterfamilias had the right to disown or sell into slavery children who displeased him, and he could legally kill his own children for angering him. The paterfamilias also determined the fate of newborns in the family. Newborns were placed on the ground. If the paterfamilias picked up the baby, the family accepted the child. If he chose not to keep the baby— usually because it was deformed, because it was a girl, or because the paterfamilias felt he could not support any more children—the family left the child outside, usually to be picked up by a passerby and raised as a slave.

The Julian Calendar

By order of Julius Caesar, the Romans devised a calendar—the Julian calendar—with 365 and a quarter days divided into 12 months and weeks with seven days. Before its creation, people throughout the region used hundreds of dating systems. The month of July was named in honor of Caesar, and it was given 31 days to signify the month's importance. Saturday derives its name from Saturn, the god of fertility and planting. January is named after Janus, the god of new beginnings. August gets its name from Emperor Augustus. August was also changed to 31 days, by taking a day from February.

The Julian calendar lasted until 1580 CE, when it was discovered that the calendar was ten days off because the 365.25 days per year was just slightly longer—by 11 minutes and 14 seconds— than the solar year. Over the years, this added up, resulting in the ten-day difference. In 1582, Pope Gregory XIII corrected the calendar, ushering in the era of the Gregorian calendar. However, the months, days of the week, and basic structure of the calendar remained intact and are still used today.

The oldest woman in a family was the materfamilias, "mother of the family." She had no legal power in the family, but she had considerable influence. The materfamilias ran the household and supported her husband's career. She was expected to conduct herself with dignity and grace.

MARRIAGE AND DIVORCE

Often, girls married as young as 12 years old. Typically, the husband was in his mid-20s. Marriages were arranged for political benefit—often, the couple did not meet prior to the wedding.

Ancient Rome had two principal kinds of marriage during the years of the republic. If a man married a woman *cum manu*, "with the hand," he had complete legal power over her and her possessions. If a man married a woman *sine manu*, "without the hand," his father-in-law maintained power over his wife and her property. Regardless of which type of marriage a woman was in, she was unable to carry out business in her name. Gradually, the position of women shifted. Fearing the upper-class population was beginning to dwindle, Augustus encouraged childbirth and rewarded women for having at least three children with *ius trium liberorum*, "the right of three." This law granted mothers with three or more children the right to conduct business for themselves.

Divorce was common, especially among patricians. A divorced woman returned to her father's care. She was able to remarry unless she had been unfaithful to her husband.

ROMAN CHILDREN

Mothers educated children at home until they were six or seven years old. Boys and some girls would then attend a private school or continue studying at home either under the guidance of their mother or with a tutor, if the family was able to afford one, until approximately age 11. Well-educated Greek slaves taught children in wealthy homes. Students learned reading, writing, and mathematics. Patrician children continued their education from ages 11 to approximately 14, learning Latin and Greek grammar and literature, music, astronomy, and mathematics. For most students, education ended at approximately age 14. Some went on to higher education, studying public speaking and debate, philosophy, and history. This would prepare them for a future in the Roman Senate.

When not studying, Roman children played a variety of games. Ball games were popular as well as marbles and an early form of jacks that used sheep knucklebones. Dolls were a favorite pastime, too. Girls had dolls made of ivory and bone, and boys played with gladiator and soldier dolls.

HOUSE AND HOME

Most of Rome's population lived in a *domus* or *insula*. A domus was a house built around a central courtyard with a pool used for collecting rainwater. An insula was a rented apartment built in a tenement block. As Rome grew, more and more insulae were made cheaply of wood and masonry and built taller and taller to house more people. Droves of Romans crowded into cramped quarters with narrow alleyways. Fire and collapse were a constant threat. Common people did not cook in their homes but in the streets. Residents had to fetch water from public fountains.

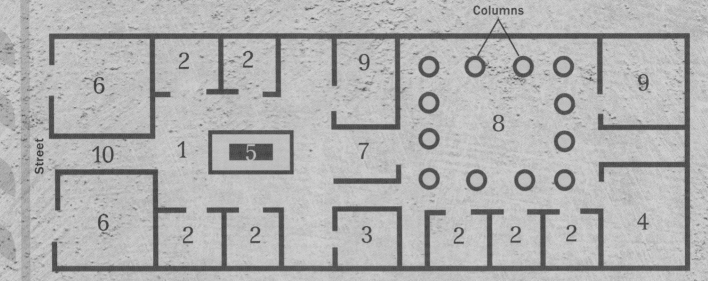

1	atrium	formal entrance hall
2	cubiculum	bedroom
3	culina	kitchen
4	exedra	garden room
5	impluvium	rainwater collecting pool
6	taberna	shop
7	tablinum	office
8	peristylium	garden
9	triclinium	dining room
10	vestibulum	entrance

By the 300s CE, almost 1 million people, not counting slaves, filled 44,000 insulae and 1,800 domus in the city of Rome.[1] Men held jobs as bath attendants, butchers, fishmongers, fruit sellers, or shopkeepers. Plebeian women worked these same jobs or labored as midwives or dressmakers.

Life was less crowded in the country. Wealthy landowners lived in villas. These large houses had many rooms. In addition to typical Roman furnishings, such as tables, beds, and crockery, villas also had small decorative tables, chests, and candelabras. Intricate mosaics or frescoes provided decoration. The front door opened into an atrium, which had an open ceiling and a pool in the middle of the floor. Many slaves lived with the family to help run the household. They bathed and dressed the family members, cared for the children, worked the land, and cooked.

Plebeian country dwellers had modest homes or lived in poverty. They farmed the fields, tending their own small parcel of land or working for wealthy landowners. They did not have lavish furnishings, and children were expected to help farm. Gardening was common. Romans often grew vegetables. The very wealthy kept exotic plants as well.

A typical Roman house often had shops on its outer wall facing the street. It centered around gardens, including a pool to collect rainwater.

FOOD

The wealthy had a diverse diet and plenty of rich foods. The main meal of the day, called *cena*, began in the afternoon and lasted for several hours. Guests often attended these dinner parties. Participants ate up to seven courses, usually while lounging on cushioned couches. Meals often included fish, poultry, and meat. Sweeter offerings included fruit and cakes. Wine was always served during the different courses.

Bathhouses and Toilets

Few homes in ancient Rome had a bath, so Romans bathed in large public bathhouses. Every town or city had a bathhouse for the locals. More than a place to wash, Roman baths were a place to relax and socialize. Romans—rich and poor, old and young—mingled at bathhouses. Women attended in the morning. Men bathed in the afternoon or evening. The bathhouse had water of different temperatures. Several furnaces—up to 50—provided hot water and steam to some baths.

Large changing rooms provided a place for patrons to undress and leave their clothing on shelves.

Bathers could then go to an exercise room. Boxing and wrestling were popular for men. Next, bathers entered a room similar to a steam room and covered their bodies with scented olive oil. Slaves used a hooked metal tool called a strigil to scrape off the oil, dirt, and sweat and performed massages. The last step in the lengthy Roman bath was a plunge into cold water.

People also shared toilets. Communal open-air toilets allowed people to sit side by side on marble seats. Running water under the bench of seats washed away the waste.

Hosts used expensive dinnerware and serving pieces made of gold, glass, and bronze to impress guests. Slaves provided entertainment in a variety of forms, including dance, musical performances, acrobatics, or juggling.

Working-class Romans did not enjoy such an extravagant diet. Their consumption of red meat was limited, and the majority of their food consisted of bread and porridge made from barley or millet rather than wheat, which was expensive. They also ate vegetables, seafood, and a fermented fish sauce called *garum*. As the population swelled, the state began distributing free grain to its citizens, which became a vital source of nutrition for the urban poor.

FASHION

Fashion was just as important as food to the patricians. Both men and women wore a tunic. Aristocratic men wore a toga. This semi-circular piece of fabric was large, measuring up to 18 feet (6 m) long and 6 feet (2 m) wide.[2] Wealthy women covered their tunics with a palla, draping and wrapping the piece of rectangular-shaped fabric like a toga. Slaves would tightly wrap the palla, making it difficult for their mistress to use her arms and hands.

Theater

Romans enjoyed Greek theater. Actors performed plays that had been translated from Greek into Latin. Actors wore clay masks during performances, which took place in small wooden theaters. By 11 BCE, Emperor Augustus built a theater that held 14,000 people called the *Theatrum Marcelli*, "Theater of Marcellus."[3]

This style was a status symbol, indicating she did not have to work with her hands and had slaves to work for her and dress her.

Wealthy Roman women had an *ornatrix*, or hairdresser. This slave would apply cosmetics and arrange the hair in intricate styles. Early cosmetics included chalk or lead foundation to lighten the skin, soot eyeliner, and wine for coloring lips and cheeks. Some of the more lavish hairstyles over the centuries involved high piles of curls atop the head. Beginning in the first century BCE, wigs made from blonde hair taken from female German slaves and black wigs made from hair from India became fashionable and highly prized. Patrician women completed their dress with several pieces of precious gemstone jewelry.

Working class and poorer Romans typically wore tunics made of whatever fabric was available. Often, their clothing was darker and duller in color.

ENTERTAINMENT

For enjoyment, Romans liked to visit the amphitheater. There, gladiators fought, sometimes to the death, as crowds cheered. The emperor hosted gladiatorial games, which were expensive. He also decided if a gladiator, who was usually a slave or a criminal, would live or die at the end of a battle if he or she had not been killed during the fight. Gladiators—men and sometimes

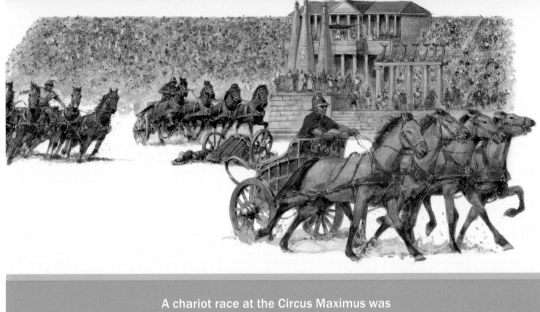

A chariot race at the Circus Maximus was a popular form of entertainment in the city of Rome.

women—fought each other using swords, spears, nets, and tridents. They had varying types of armor. Sometimes, the gladiators also had to fight wild animals such as leopards, bears, tigers, and lions. The Colosseum, Rome's largest amphitheater, could seat more than 50,000 spectators, who gladly packed themselves into its rows to watch the show.[4]

Chariot races were popular, too. Charioteers would race on a circus. The most famous of these tracks, the Circus Maximus in the city of Rome, could hold 250,000 people.[5] Chariots would race the length of the track, which was 2,000 feet (610 m), turn around posts at the end, and race back.[6] Races were typically seven laps. Winners received palm branches, which symbolized victory, and prize money.

CHAPTER 5

ARCHITECTURE AND ART

In 75 CE, the Roman scholar Pliny the Elder wrote, "In great buildings as well as in other things, the rest of the world has been outdone by us Romans."[1] Two of the most significant and recognizable contributions of ancient Rome are its architecture and art. Several examples endure today. They attest to the Romans' dedication to craft, culture, and beauty.

The architecture of Rome's mighty Colosseum relies heavily on columns and arches.

GRAND DESIGN

Augustus boasted that he had transformed Rome from a city of brick into a city of marble. Predecessor Julius Caesar began quarrying gleaming white marble from the mountains of Carrara, located north of the city of Rome in modern-day Tuscany. When Augustus came to power, he sped up the work, and the Romans quarried huge quantities of marble from Carrara each year.

The ancient Romans borrowed heavily from Greek architecture but made their structures bigger and more extravagant. Of particular note is

The Dead

Romans buried their dead in tombs. Elaborate carvings, often depicting the deceased's profession, decorated tomb walls. Relief carvings show physicians working on patients, storekeepers in their shops, and bakers in front of their ovens. Altars to the dead and tombstones included carvings with names, dates, and loving sentiments.

In 2014, archaeologists discovered a cemetery in an ancient Roman port. The find, which was unearthed in the town of Ostia, had different types of funeral rites, including both burials and cremations. The differences in the burial methods point to Ostia being a multicultural town. So far, researchers have uncovered approximately a dozen tombs, along with lead tablets with inscriptions carved into them meant to curse any looters. The cemetery in Ostia, which dates back 2,700 years, is extraordinary because it shows that ancient people living in the town had the freedom to decide what would become of their bodies when they died.

the column, which the Romans used heavily in their architecture. Columns can support the weight of other structural elements or simply provide decoration. The Romans took the Doric, Corinthian, and Ionic styles from the Greeks. Doric columns are smooth or fluted, with grooves. Corinthian style is more ornate than Doric, with intricately carved acanthus leaves and scrolls. The Ionic design features scrollwork at the top. The Doric and the Ionic feature fluted sides down the length of the columns, though the grooves are thinner, with 24 flutes to the Doric style's 20 flutes. The Colosseum has all three styles, with Doric on the first floor, Ionic on the second floor, and Corinthian on the third floor.

Roman architects had a broad array of skills. They used elements of construction engineering, civil engineering, mechanical engineering, urban planning, and construction management. They were also ahead of their time in terms of harmonizing various elements of construction planning. Aesthetics played an important part in Roman architecture. Marcus Vitruvius Pollio, who lived during the first century BCE, is credited as the father of architectural acoustics, or the way sound carries in a room's design. He wrote a groundbreaking treatise on architecture, and his work helped transform the art into a professional discipline.

THE COLOSSEUM

One of the most recognized examples of ancient Roman architecture remains today. The ruins of the once mighty Colosseum still stand in the center of Rome. The mammoth arena, officially named the Flavian Amphitheater, was one of Rome's finest examples of engineering and architecture.

Emperor Vespasian commissioned the Colosseum in approximately 70 CE. It opened in 80 CE, during the reign of Titus, Vespasian's son. The four-story oval amphitheater measures 620 feet (189 m) long, 513 feet (156 m) wide, and 157 feet (48 m) high.[2] Made of stone and concrete, with three stories of arched entrances, it could hold 50,000 spectators.[3] Passages and chambers beneath the arena floor transported and held gladiators and animals.

The Colosseum was used for gladiator battles, wild animal fights, and mock naval engagements for more than four centuries before falling into neglect. Subsequent residents plundered stones from the structure for building materials. The Colosseum also

Dozens of Amphitheaters

More than 200 amphitheaters still exist across what was once the Roman Empire. Examples include the remains of Caesarea in Israel and the ruins of Aquincum in Budapest, Hungary. And the partially preserved Chester Roman Amphitheatre in Great Britain once held 8,000 to 12,000 spectators.[4]

endured earthquakes, lightning strikes, and vandalism. Today, one-third of the original structure remains.

THE PANTHEON

The Pantheon is the best-preserved building of ancient Rome. More than 2,000 years old, it is a marvel of Roman architecture and construction. This domed building measures almost 142 feet (43 m) in diameter and 142 feet (43 m) high.[5] The Romans constructed it with brick and concrete in the city of Rome in approximately the 120s CE to replace a previous Pantheon, which burned to the ground in 80 CE.

The Pantheon has a series of intersecting arches, piers, and supports. Additional arches that run horizontally around the Pantheon support the dome. The arches helped sustain the weight of building materials, and builders used lighter materials toward the top of the dome to allow the arches to support the dome's sheer size. The rotunda is perfectly round, another architectural feat for ancient Roman builders. Only the front portico, which serves as an entrance, is rectangular.

The oculus is an opening in the middle of the dome. It is 30 feet (9 m) in diameter.[6] Sunlight pours through the oculus, lighting the Pantheon's beautiful interior. Since its construction, the Pantheon has been used as a temple to the Roman gods, a Christian church, a national shrine, and a burial

place for famous Italians, including the Renaissance painter Raphael from the 1400s CE.

SCULPTURE

Romans were quite fond of art and admired Greek creations. After conquering Greece in the 140s BCE and studying Greek styles, sculptors and painters copied Greek art techniques. Many artists in Rome were Greeks who had moved there, where they thrived due to the high demand for their work.

While Roman sculptors admired the Greek classical style, they did not simply copy it. The Greeks strived for ideal portrayals of their subjects. Roman sculptors made the Greek style their own by creating realistic portraits of their subjects that conveyed facial details and personalities. Roman

Sunshine streams through the oculus of the Pantheon, a popular tourist attraction.

sculptors incorporated physical peculiarities and defects of their subjects, resulting in truer-to-life works. Artists worked with stone, precious metals, glass, and terra-cotta, saving bronze and marble for the finest, most distinguished works. Sculptors created large pieces in the likeness of emperors and important people. These artists also carved smaller busts and miniaturized copies of Greek statues. Sculptures adorned the homes of the wealthy and public spaces, such as bathhouses and fountains.

One famous example is a bronze statue of Emperor Marcus Aurelius, which was dedicated

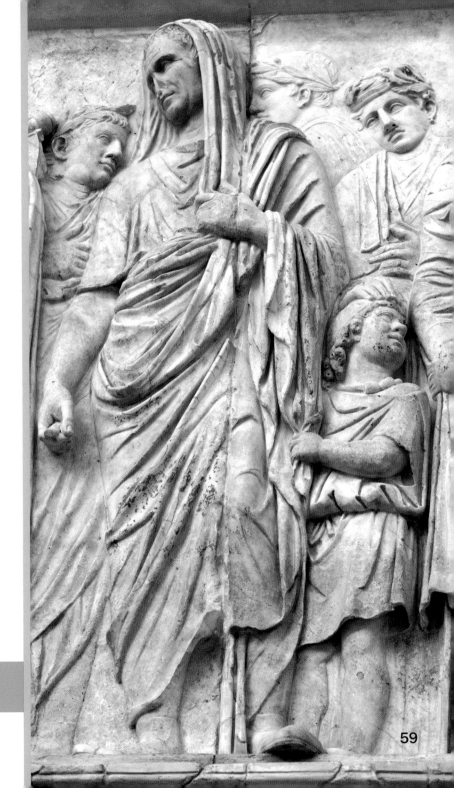

Members of Emperor Augustus's family appear to emerge from the stone in the *Ara Pacis* monument in Rome.

in 175 CE. It is 11.5 feet (3.5 m) high and shows the ruler atop his horse.[7] The statue was originally covered in gold leaf and is in the Capitoline Museums in Rome. A replica stands in the city's Piazza del Campidoglio.

Sculptures also depicted historical events. For these, sculptors used relief carving, a Roman innovation. The technique involves carving away a flat surface to give the illusion that the scene is raised above or coming out of the background. These carvings often occupied large public monuments, columns, and triumphal arches.

Emperors had several statues of themselves made to send to cities within the empire that were far from Rome. People living in conquered lands could see what their new ruler looked like. Many of these works of art exist today.

FRESCOES AND MOSAICS

The rich adorned their homes with paintings and mosaics. Archaeologists have uncovered frescoes in many excavated ancient Roman homes, including those in Pompeii. Artists painted vivid and realistic scenes on the interiors of private homes in Roman cities as well as in the country. Pliny the Elder wrote at the time that the subjects of fresco paintings could be such things as "villas, porticos, landscape gardens, woods, groves, hills, pools, channels, rivers, and coastlines."[8] Because most Roman homes lacked

Frescoes at Pompeii survived the eruption of Vesuvius.

windows, frescoes helped to brighten and enliven the interior walls with outdoor scenes.

One of the most abundant forms of art that remains from ancient Rome is the mosaic. Some mosaics were very detailed and often depicted intricate designs. Both paintings and mosaics helped make Roman rooms seem larger and more inviting. These works of art also showed off the wealth of the home's owner. So many mosaics are known today because floors, which were often mosaic, are usually the only part of Roman buildings that survive.

CHAPTER 6

GODS AND GODDESSES

Religion was an important aspect of daily life in Rome. The Romans worshiped several gods and goddesses, whom they thought controlled the lives of humans and natural events. The Romans took care not to anger the gods, believing that doing so could lead to earthquakes, fires, volcanic eruptions, or other destruction.

Neptune was the Roman god of the sea.

WORSHIP

Jupiter was the most important Roman god. He was the king of the gods and ruled with his wife, Juno, the goddess of the sky. Mars was the god of war. The Romans considered him quite powerful, too. Neptune was the god of the sea. If a ship hit a violent storm at sea, the Romans believed Neptune was not happy with them.

Romans built temples and shrines in honor of their gods. Every Roman city had a temple devoted to three divine beings: Jupiter, Juno, and Minerva,

Important Roman Gods and Goddesses

Apollo	God of music, light, and truth	Minerva	Goddess of wisdom and the arts
Ceres	Goddess of agriculture	Neptune	God of the sea
Diana	Goddess of fertility and hunting	Pluto	God of the underworld
Juno	Queen of the gods, and goddess of marriage	Saturn	God of agriculture
Jupiter	King of the gods, and god of the sky and thunder	Venus	Goddess of love and beauty
Mars	God of war	Vesta	Goddess of the hearth and home
Mercury	God of trade, merchants, and travelers	Vulcan	God of fire

the goddess of wisdom and the arts. The Romans referred to them collectively as the Capitoline Triad.

The ancient Romans also honored their gods with special festival days. Romans visited the temple of the god or goddess being celebrated that day. Temple priests burned incense and sacrificed animals as offerings to that god or goddess.

The Romans built temples throughout the empire, usually in a similar pattern. A triangular-shaped roof sat atop great pillars, and steps led to a main doorway. A statue of the god or goddess of the temple stood inside. Priests used outdoor altars for animal sacrifices. Augurs inside the temples practiced divination by looking for signs in the entrails of the sacrificed animals or in the flight patterns of birds. Augurs also attempted to examine the will of the gods to ward off their anger, which would avoid natural disasters. Romans took the predictions of augurs very seriously and used remedies to deal with portents. Some people in ancient Rome used astrology to predict the future.

Temple of Vesta

Near the Roman Forum was the Temple of Vesta, honoring the goddess of the hearth and home. Many cities had a temple to Vesta. Priestesses known as vestal virgins ran the temple. Their duty was to ensure the sacred fire inside the temple did not go out. They were not allowed to marry and bear children while serving as priestesses, and they took a vow of chastity. Should a priestess break that vow, the punishment was being buried alive. All aspects of their lives were devoted to the rituals associated with Vesta. Six girls served simultaneously, each for 30 years.[1] After serving, vestal virgins could marry and have children. They could also conduct their own business and lived in luxurious accommodations at the expense of the state.

Roman homes had a small altar and shrine to worship their personal household gods or spirits. These were called Lares. The paterfamilias would lead the family and slaves in daily prayers around the shrine.

RELIGION AND GOVERNMENT

The state controlled religion. Priests were elected or appointed to their office, which made them government officials. Their sacrifices to appease the gods were not simply for the worshipers but to win the favor of the gods for the state of Rome. Although Romans believed in an afterlife, the Roman government did not view religion as something to meet a spiritual need or offer salvation and consolation for the individual. Rather, religion focused on loyalty to the gods, who defended the Roman res publica.

Pontiffs were the most important priests, a title later used in the Catholic Church to signify the Pope. The highest priest was the *Pontifex Maximus*, a position held by the emperor during the Roman Empire.

Gods were not simply unseen beings. Rulers were often deified, or declared gods. Emperors Augustus, Claudius, Vespasian, Titus, Hadrian, and Antoninus Pius were all honored as gods after their deaths. Romans worshiped them along with the other Roman gods, though the people did not revere the former rulers as highly as gods such as Jupiter. Some emperors, such as Caligula and Domitian, portrayed themselves as gods while they were still alive. Such actions were met with fierce resistance.

THE GODS OF OTHER LANDS

As the Roman Empire pushed into new lands, the Romans discovered the religions of other cultures and incorporated them into the Roman religion. The Romans were introduced to the gods of Egypt, Phrygia (modern-day Turkey), Britain, and the East.

Rome's rule included Judaea, at the eastern end of the Mediterranean. Jews lived there. They believed in one god. Worshiping any other gods or human beings was against their beliefs. Some Roman emperors were tolerant of the Jews' refusal to worship Roman gods, but other emperors were not.

Jesus, or Jesus Christ, who lived in Judaea, was a Jewish holy man believed to be the son of the Jews' God. He attracted a large following of believers, who considered him to be the long-awaited savior sent by God. Those who believed in Jesus would be granted eternal life after death.

Admiring the Egyptians

The Romans were intrigued by the practice of mummification in Egypt and some Romans living in Egypt adopted it. They took Egyptian obelisks to Rome. The Egyptians had built the tall, four-sided, narrow tapering monuments in honor of their sun god Re, also known as Ra. Romans used the obelisks to decorate public spaces and racetracks.

Some Roman rulers considered Jesus a threat. Some Jews despised him, too, not believing he was the true son of God. In approximately 30 CE, the Roman governor Pontius Pilate had Jesus crucified, which was often reserved for non-Roman criminals, slaves, and rebels. During a crucifixion, the Romans nailed the person to a large wooden cross and left him or her to die an agonizing death that could take hours, sometimes days. Roman citizens condemned to death for crimes, on the other hand, died quickly and cleanly by decapitation.

After Jesus's death, Paul of Tarsus, one of his disciples, carried on with spreading the Jewish religion to non-Jews within the Roman Empire. Officials arrested Paul, a Roman citizen, and held him in Rome. They put him to death in approximately 64 CE, under the rule of Emperor Nero. Nero blamed Christianity, named after Jesus Christ, for social disruption and ordered the destruction of Christian churches.

CHRISTIANITY SPREADS

The deaths of Jesus Christ and Paul did not end the spread of Christianity. Those who followed Jesus became known as Christians. Christianity spread throughout the empire. Many Romans viewed the Christians' refusal to worship Roman gods as treason.

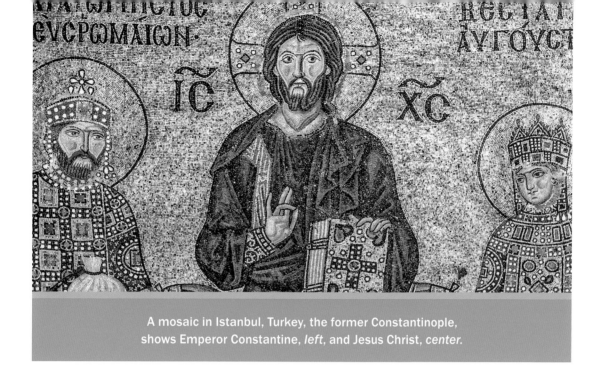

A mosaic in Istanbul, Turkey, the former Constantinople, shows Emperor Constantine, *left*, and Jesus Christ, *center*.

By the 300s CE, however, Christianity was the main religion of the Roman Empire. Emperor Constantine, who became one of two emperors beginning in 312, was a Christian. He went on to rule the Roman Empire solo in 324 and did everything in his power to spread Christianity throughout the empire. He founded Constantinople in the East, a Christian capital he named for himself, and filled it with churches. While Constantine made Christianity a state religion, he also allowed paganism. Many Roman citizens converted to their emperor's faith, and Christianity spread faster. In 380, Theodosius I made Christianity the religion of the empire. When the Roman Empire finally fell, Christianity continued and spread.

CHAPTER 7

BUILDERS AND CRAFTSMEN

While much of the architecture from ancient Rome has crumbled into ruin, a number of buildings, bridges, roads, and monuments remain today. These structures stand as a testament to the engineering and building abilities of the ancient Romans.

In Segovia, Spain, a Roman aqueduct still towers dozens of feet above the city's people and buildings.

AQUEDUCTS AND SEWER SYSTEMS

Perhaps the greatest example of Roman engineering was the widespread use of aqueducts. These artificial channels moved water. Some aqueducts were tunnels through rocks or canals in the earth. Others looked like bridges, with channels that carried water above ground. Aqueducts used gravity to move the water supply.

Ancient Rome's aqueducts were nothing short of an engineering marvel. First century BCE Rome had a population of almost 1 million people.[1] Waste became a huge problem. Garbage, human and animal waste, used cooking and cleaning water, and any other refuse became an issue. The Tiber River, Rome's only source of clean water, soon became polluted and choked with garbage, human waste, and even dead bodies.

In 33 BCE, Marcus Agrippa became water commissioner. By the end of the first century, the Romans had built nine aqueducts that carried 85 million gallons (322 million L) of fresh mountain spring water into Rome each day.[2] The Aqua Claudia supplied Rome from a water source 42 miles (68 km) away.[3] It carried freshwater to Rome's 14 districts. Aqueducts delivered water to public bathhouses and to fountains, where residents could collect the water.

The aqueducts serving Rome with freshwater comprised an extensive network of arches, channels, and tunnels. The Romans did not invent the aqueduct, but Roman engineers combined reservoir construction, bridge building, tunneling, piping, and road making to create a state-of-the-art water delivery system. Wherever possible, aqueducts carried water underground or through tunnels or channels to protect the water from contamination. People still use some of the aqueducts today.

A system of sewers covered by stones removed wastewater. Human waste was flushed from the public latrines into a channel that fed into the main sewage system. This emptied into a nearby river or stream.

CONCRETE AND ARCHES

Arguably the most important contribution Rome made to the field of architecture was the invention of concrete. For a long time, Romans had been using mortar to hold building blocks together. More than 2,100 years ago, Romans began mixing aggregate into their mortar to create concrete. They used the material to create aqueducts, buildings, bridges, and monuments. The addition of volcanic ash called pozzolana, which was

Vitruvius

Marcus Vitruvius Pollio, known simply as Vitruvius, was a Roman civil engineer, architect, and author who lived during the first century BCE. Scholars remember Vitruvius for his written works, a collection of volumes called *De Architectura*. It is one of the most important sources of knowledge about Roman building methods. In it, Vitruvius described the planning and design of structures such as aqueducts and baths, as well as machinery, measuring devices, and instruments.

plentiful in the area, created a sticky paste that was strong enough to endure decay or crumbling. The Roman scholar Pliny the Elder, who died in the eruption of Vesuvius in 79 CE, wrote about pozzolana being used to make a special maritime concrete that could set and harden under water for use in piers and harbors.

Concrete allowed Roman builders to make tenement buildings, bridges, and arches sturdier than before. Roman builders grew more knowledgeable about concrete's uses. Their understanding allowed for the successful

Tracking Time

The Romans used sundials to gauge how far along in the day it was and water clocks to act as early stopwatches. The Solarium Augusti in Rome was a large obelisk that cast a shadow, based on the sun's position, onto pavement inlaid with gilded bronze lines. One could read the time based on where the shadow fell among the lines.

Water clocks, called clepsydras, used a regulated flow of liquid into or out of a vessel. Often, a clepsydra was a small earthenware vessel that had a hole in its side, close to the base. Wax was used to plug the hole. When a person wanted to start marking time, they poured water into the vessel and pulled out the wax plug. The water began to flow out of the clepsydra. Once the vessel was empty, time was up. The amount of allotted time was based on how much water was poured into the vessel. For example, the Romans used them in court to allow speakers a certain amount of time to present their cases. As time passed, water clocks became more intricate, with small wheels connected to hands on a dial that turned as water dripped onto them.

construction of the Pantheon in the 100s CE. The seven-story structure remains intact, crowned with the largest unsupported concrete dome existing in the world today.

The Pantheon also shows the usefulness of arches. The Romans discovered that arches put much less strain on stone blocks than the traditional stacking of bricks. This made arches a far more efficient building technique. Arches could create tall, strong walls and doorways as well as domes and vaults. The Romans incorporated arches in a variety of structures, including aqueducts.

HYPOCAUST

Romans also mastered the art of central heating, which they called hypocaust. They used it in houses and public bathhouses.

Slaves kept a furnace fire blazing, which heated the air. The warm air passed through spaces builders created under floors and between walls. Hypocaust was so effective that people in some homes had to wear wooden shoes to avoid burning their feet on the hot floor.

Hypocaust also allowed for hot water baths and saunas in public bathhouses. Water could be heated hot enough to produce steam for steam rooms.

SUPERIOR ROADS

Roadways in the ancient world were rarely more than heavily traveled paths. Rain made them muddy. Deep ruts and holes were constant problems, leading to broken cart wheels. The Romans changed that, devising a system for building roads that drastically improved transportation throughout the empire.

The Romans laid out roads as straight as possible. Surveyors used a tool called a *groma* to ensure the planned paths were straight by plotting right angles. The first major Roman military highway was the Appian Way. The Romans named it after Appius Claudius Caecus, the Roman official who began its construction in 312 BCE. Initially 132 miles (212 km) long and extending from the city of Rome to Capua, the Romans extended it an additional 234 miles (377 km) to Italy's southeast coast.[4]

Workers began by clearing land, including chopping down trees. Next, they dug trenches: a wide one for the road, with one on each side for drainage. Then, they filled the road trench with layers of materials that varied given what was available. First was compacted sand or earth,

Groma

The *groma* was an instrument using lead weights that surveyors used to create straight roads. The Latin word for *lead* is *plumbum*, which led to "plumb line," a term for a tool people use today to check that something is level.

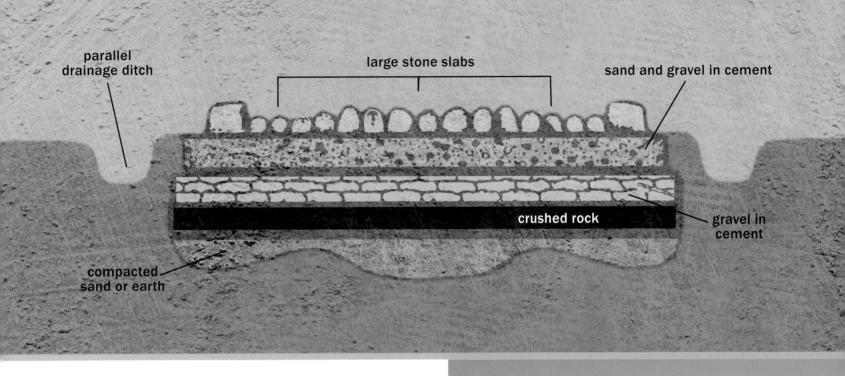

parallel drainage ditch

large stone slabs

sand and gravel in cement

crushed rock

gravel in cement

compacted sand or earth

The Romans perfected their formula for building roads.

followed by crushed rock. Next was gravel, which eventually was mixed in cement. Workers added a layer of sand and gravel next, also mixed with cement. The top was usually large stone slabs.

Over time, the Romans created 50,000 miles (80,000 km) of roads.[5] The routes allowed Roman armies to travel quickly and efficiently. Farmers and traders pulling crops and goods by oxcart also benefitted. Many of these roads, including the Appian Way, still exist today.

METALWORK AND GLASSBLOWING

Nearly every Roman city had a blacksmith who was skilled in ironwork, a craft the Romans did not invent but were quite adept at. The blacksmith used a furnace, anvil, hammer, and pincers to hammer pots and tools into shape.

Bronzesmiths were also active in ancient Rome. They created bronze objects by casting. First, they made a wax model of an object and covered it in clay. Next, they heated the clay until the wax melted and could be poured out of the clay, leaving behind a mold. The bronzesmith could then pour molten bronze into the mold. Once fully set, the clay cast could be broken, revealing the bronze object inside.

Romans also produced glass. They created an enormous number of blown glass vessels, containers, dishes, and other items using a mixture of silica, soda, and lime heated in a furnace to more than 2,000 degrees Fahrenheit (1,000°C). Glassblowers shaped molten glass using a hollow metal tube through which they blew air into a blob of the material attached at the other end. The Romans did not invent glass, but they were the first to implement its widespread use in windows.

Roman artisans created glass vessels in a variety of shapes, sizes, and colors.

CHAPTER 8

MIGHT OF THE LEGIONS

Warfare in ancient Rome was essentially an instrument of expansion. The Roman army was one of the most successful in the history of the world. Rome's military strength allowed the empire to spread to three continents. Rome's soldiers established Roman rule with great precision.

A Roman relief shows Roman soldiers.

SERVING IN THE ARMY

During the days of the Roman monarchy and then the republic, men served in the Roman army for only part of the year. They were not paid. Rather, the government expected them to serve out of a sense of duty. The army was called together for a season of campaigning, pushing into new lands. Men then returned home in time to harvest their crops and, therefore, did not generally lose money by serving in the army. Sometimes, wars would last longer than one season, so soldiers were forced to remain with the army through the winter. One of the first written accounts of soldiers receiving pay for military service was during the siege of the Etruscan city of Veii, which lasted ten years, from 406 to 396 BCE.

By the first century BCE, Rome's army had shifted from a part-time military comprised of volunteers to a professional standing army of men who received regular pay for their service. Officers received much higher pay than soldiers. The highest-ranking centurions made more than 133 times the salary of a legionnaire.[1]

Many soldiers in the Roman army saw themselves as superior to members of the civilian population. Records indicate that civilians often feared running into soldiers, who were known to bully them or forcibly take their pack animals. Extortion was also common. Soldiers would demand sums of money from business owners and threaten to harm them if they did not comply.

Upon retirement, if a soldier survived that long, every legionnaire was given a plot of land to farm. During the reign of Tiberius, in 14 CE, Rome had trouble honoring the promise of providing land to retiring legionnaires.

Roman Medicine

Physicians in the Roman army carried a host of medical instruments that could be used to close wounds, set bones, and create artificial limbs from wood and bronze. Their medical kit included tools for extracting arrows, as well as forceps, scalpels, and catheters, which they would disinfect with boiling water. Doctors administered painkillers, such as opium, and cleaned out wounds using acid vinegar. They also had a variety of herbal remedies, such as fennel for nervous disorders, and they used boiled liver for eye sores.

The Roman army battlefield was the birthplace of the hospital. The Romans placed injured soldiers together in a barrack, where a physician closely monitored them. The Romans were already aware of the connection between mosquitoes and human diseases, and they were careful not to set up hospitals near swamps, where the insects thrive.

Although Roman physicians were not allowed to dissect human corpses to study the human body, they did remarkably well with some surgeries and procedures. Roman physicians were adept at cataract surgery and trepanation, which was drilling a hole in the skull. Romans believed this treatment relieved pain in the head caused by wounds or disease.

When younger soldiers heard about the plight of their older retiring comrades, mutiny broke out.

Tiberius realized he needed the army to maintain his rule and sent his nephew and adopted son, Germanicus, to quell the upheaval. Germanicus was a popular and well-respected general. He effectively restored peace. In the process, Tiberius learned an important lesson: the very existence of the empire depended upon the loyalty of the Roman army.

LEGIONS OF SOLDIERS

Rome's earliest armies, prior to approximately 550 BCE, consisted of men from neighboring tribes banding together in groups when threatened by a common enemy. Then, in approximately 550 BCE, King Servius Tullius implemented the mandatory service of eligible men in the military when war called for it. As time went on, the army became more structured, more heavily armed, and a more powerful force.

Rome's army consisted of three groups: legions, auxiliaries, and the Praetorian Guard. Each legion had approximately 5,000 men and included soldiers, doctors, surveyors, and engineers.[2] These men were called legionnaires. They carried out military campaigns and also built roads, walls, aqueducts, and tunnels. All members of the Roman legion had to be Roman

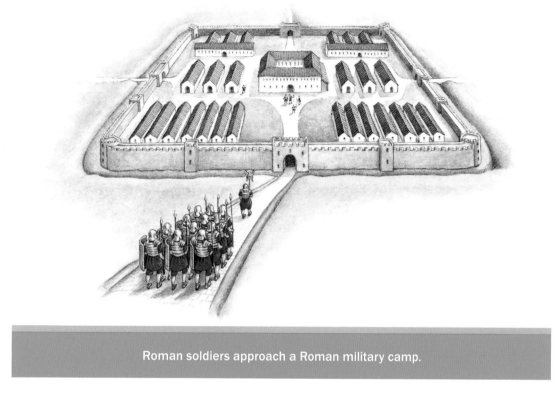

citizens to be eligible for service. Under Augustus, the Roman army could field 23 legions.[3]

Noncitizens of Rome comprised the auxiliaries, which fought with the legionnaires. Auxiliaries were lightly armed and fought as specialized troops—often with bows or slings—or as cavalrymen. Rome granted auxiliaries citizenship when they retired from the army.

The Praetorian Guard consisted of an elite group of Roman soldiers who served as the emperor's bodyguards. Unlike other Roman soldiers who were sent on military campaigns far and wide, the Praetorian Guard remained in the city of Rome. The guard began with approximately 9,000 men and varied in size over time.[4]

Most of Rome's soldiers were professionals and served in the army for 25 years. They were highly trained and could employ different battle tactics in response to trumpet signals. Soldiers had incredible stamina for marching great distances, were skilled at fighting in precise formation, and could kill expertly and efficiently.

Legions were divided into ten cohorts, or divisions. These were further broken down into units called centuries. An officer called a centurion led each century.

Roman legionnaires were heavily armed and protected. An iron helmet protected the head and face. Legionnaires wore armor of overlapping metal strips, held together with leather strips over a red tunic. A legionnaire carried two pila. These were javelins with long iron heads that could be thrown at the enemy. A soldier also had a *gladius*, a short sword for hand-to-hand combat. Additionally, Roman legionnaires carried curved shields called

Military Camps

As legions of Roman soldiers marched into new lands, they stopped at night and set up camp. All Roman legions erected camp in the same layout. The rectangular scheme had soldiers' and officers' tents arranged in rows. The general's quarters and the camp headquarters were in the interior. A soldier could enter another legion's camp and know exactly where everything was because of the uniform layout of the Roman army camp.

scuta. Groups of legionnaires could raise their *scuta* flat above their heads in a formation called *testudo*, tortoise. With their shields interlocked in a massive barrier above them like the shell of a turtle, they could advance against well-defended enemies and forts, avoiding harm from arrows or other items thrown down on them.

THE ARMY OF TRAJAN

Trajan was one of many Roman generals who went on to become emperor, reigning from 98 to 117 CE. He led his armies as far north as the Danube River in present-day Germany and as far east as present-day Iraq. He was so popular with his troops that Emperor Nerva decided to name him as his successor.

Trajan's conquests brought great wealth to Rome. Conquered areas of Dacia (modern-day Romania), Arabia, and Parthia (modern-day Iran), provided ore, grain, and livestock to the empire.

But the military accomplishments of Trajan's men were not without hardships. Soldiers had to march great distances, cross rivers, build camps, forage for food, and fight bravely for these conquests. Rome erected a marble column in honor of Trajan and his legions, complete with reliefs showing Trajan's military campaigns.

A CLOSER LOOK

TRAJAN'S COLUMN

Completed in 113 CE, Trajan's Column stands 125 feet (38 m) tall.[5] The monument, which still stands today in Trajan's Forum in Rome, consists of white Italian Carrara marble drums, each weighing approximately 32 short tons (29 metric tons).[6] Carvings in the marble pillar depict the events of the Dacian Wars in which Trajan and his army were victorious. One long continuous carving, called a frieze, wraps up and around the shaft of the column. Images include the Roman army preparing for battle and fighting the enemy and Emperor Trajan addressing his troops. Trajan appears 59 times.[7] The column serves as a record of Roman military arms and methods of warfare.

Inside the column, a spiral staircase winds up the interior. Outside, a gilded statue of Trajan tops the monument. The beautifully carved column still stands as a testament to both the military success and the artistic ability of the ancient Romans.

CHAPTER 9

THE LEGACY OF ROME

Approximately 800 years after the fall of the West Roman Empire, the Renaissance period in Europe, which began in the 1300s CE, revitalized interest in Roman architecture and art. Education emphasized Greek and Roman literature, and students began studying Latin.

A Roman aqueduct is one of Istanbul's landmarks and an undeniable example of ancient Rome's reach and skill.

The Enlightenment was a European intellectual movement that took place in the late 1600s and the 1700s. It emphasized reason and individualism rather than tradition. Studying Latin became an important aspect of training the mind for intellectual reasoning.

Although the Roman Empire collapsed more than 1,500 years ago, the legacy of Rome lives on in many aspects of daily life in numerous nations around the globe. Modern cultures, including the United States, owe much to the ancient Romans.

AN ENDURING FORM OF GOVERNMENT

The basis for the idea of the separation of powers in the US Constitution dates back to the Roman Republic. The concept of representation for the people and several aspects of the US legal system come from the Romans, including several legal terms, such as *alibi*, which literally means "elsewhere," and *pro bono*, "for the good."

The Roman philosopher and politician Cicero inspired the Founding Fathers of the United States. Thomas Jefferson cited Cicero's writings as contributing greatly to how he drafted the Declaration of Independence and shaping Americans' understanding of the right to revolt.

John Adams, another Founding Father and the second president of the United States, said, "As all the ages of the world have not produced a greater statesman and philosopher united in the same character [as Cicero], his authority should have great weight."[1] Voltaire, a French writer during the Enlightenment period, said, "The Romans had their Cicero, who alone is perhaps worth all the philosophers of Greece."[2]

LATIN LANGUAGES

The Roman Catholic Church helped preserve Latin by adopting it as the official language of the church. Although Latin was not new to many areas of Europe, as Christianity spread into France, Spain, northern Italy, Portugal, Romania, and several other areas, so did Latin, the language of the Catholic mass. From the 400s to the 900s CE, Latin evolved differently in these different regions, mixing with local languages to form unique languages with a Latin base. William the Conqueror introduced Norman French, also affected by Latin, to England in the 1000s CE. As a result, today more than half of English words are Latin in origin.

The Census

Every ten years, the US government performs a census, a count of the number of people living in the nation. This practice dates back to the Roman Republic, when the government counted and recorded adult males fit for military service. Every five years, every male Roman citizen had to travel to Rome for the census. There, he would declare his family, wife, children, and slaves and report his wealth. If he failed to register with the censor, the government could take all his possessions and make the man a slave.

Latin has an everyday presence in the United States. The Latin phrase *e pluribus unum*, which means "one out of many," is on the Great Seal of the United States and is stamped on US coins. *Annuit cœptis*, "he approves of the undertaking," and *novus ordo seclorum*, "new order of the ages," are on the US one-dollar bill.

MODERN ARCHITECTURE AND ART

The Renaissance was a cultural movement that began in Italy during the early 1300s. That time was marked by a great resurgence in ideas and the arts. Artists such as Michelangelo, Raphael, and Leonardo da Vinci created extraordinary works that returned to the classic Roman models. Many consider Michelangelo to be the greatest sculptor of all time. He mastered accurately portraying the human form. He also perfected the fresco art form with his paintings on the ceiling of the Vatican's Sistine Chapel.

Italian architect and engineer Filippo Brunelleschi revived elements of ancient Roman architecture. In 1442, work began on the Pazzi Chapel in Florence, Italy, which he designed to incorporate arches and columns.

The architecture of ancient Rome also influenced the New World. It was a major factor in the design of Washington, DC, including the US Capitol. Construction on the Capitol began in 1793. Thomas Jefferson, a Founding Father who was secretary of state at the time, had a passionate interest in

Artist Constantino Brumindi, who was born in Rome, painted the *Apotheosis of Washington*, a fresco in the US Capitol building.

architecture. He wanted the design to resemble a Roman temple. Its tall columns, triangular pediments, and domed roofs recapture the style of the grand public buildings of ancient Rome.

The US Capitol building also showcases a grand example of Roman-style art. A massive fresco on the interior of the building's dome depicts George Washington with a number of Roman gods and goddesses.

The US Supreme Court building also draws upon classical Roman architecture, with its Corinthian columns and portico. The Jefferson Memorial and the Washington Monument also have Roman architectural elements in their design. Other US structures reflect Roman influence as well, including New York City's Washington Square Arch.

Roman architectural influences can be seen in other areas of the world as well. Built between 1675 and 1710, Saint Paul's Cathedral in London, England, boasts many examples of Roman architecture. Similar to Rome's Pantheon, a huge dome rests atop eight large arches 365 feet (111 m) overhead.[3] The western entrance of the church features a portico, and the inside of the dome is adorned with frescoes and mosaics.

The Arc de Triomphe in Paris, France, is another example. Emperor Napoléon Bonaparte commissioned the structure in 1806 as a tribute to his imperial armies. Construction was completed in 1836. The arch was patterned after the great triumphal arches of ancient Rome, and at 162 feet (49 m) high, it is the tallest of its kind in the world.[4]

ROME'S LEGACY

Ancient Rome's influence is widespread and enduring. The Roman alphabet and calendar are still in use as well as countless words based in the Latin language. The underlying basis for the US legal system has ancient Rome to thank, and elements of Roman architecture dot the landscape in courthouses, libraries, museums, post offices, and town halls. The Romans founded the cities of London; Cologne, Germany; and Paris and Lyon, France. And people still use the routes established by the system of Roman roads.

People in Rome today can still enjoy the Forum.

Although the once glorious Colosseum no longer hosts displays of gladiator skills, the bullfights held in amphitheaters in Spain have endured with their Roman influences. And since the time of Emperor Constantine, Christianity, Rome's last official religion, has grown and spread throughout the world.

Physical evidence of Roman rule can be seen as far away as present-day Scotland, Egypt, and Iraq in the forms of temple ruins, roadways, monuments, bathhouses, and aqueducts. But the influence of ancient Rome has lived on and spread much farther via art, architecture, language, and religion. With all that it achieved and the scope of its influence, the world may never experience another civilization as great as that of ancient Rome.

TIMELINE

C. 1000 BCE
Small village communities along the Tiber River unite into a single settlement inhabitants call Rome.

C. 600 BCE
The Etruscans from northern Italy take control of Rome.

509 BCE
Roman nobles overthrow Lucius Tarquinius Superbus, an Etruscan king, launching the Roman Republic.

264–241 BCE
Rome fights in the First Punic War and takes Sicily as its first province.

218–201 BCE
Rome battles Carthage in the Second Punic War, during which Hannibal attacks from the north.

149–146 BCE
Rome annexes portions of northern Africa and Spain during the Third Punic War.

44 BCE
On March 15, senators murder Julius Caesar, fearing his ascent to power.

31 BCE
On September 2, Octavian becomes Rome's sole leader, the emperor, which ushers in the Roman Empire.

43 CE
Emperor Claudius pushes troops as far west as Britain and as far south as present-day Morocco and Algeria.

79
On August 24, Vesuvius erupts and destroys Pompeii and Herculaneum.

80

Rome's Colosseum opens and hosts gladiatorial games and other public events.

98–117

Under Emperor Trajan, Rome reaches its height of power, stretching across three continents.

c. 120s

The Romans complete the Pantheon, a temple.

284

Diocletian becomes emperor, then reorganizes the government and standardizes Roman coins.

395

The sons of Emperor Theodosius I, Arcadius and Honorius, split the Roman Empire in two: West and East.

410

The Visigoths, a Germanic group, sack the city of Rome and leave.

476

Germanic leader Odoacer and his army defeat the West Roman Empire.

1453

The Ottomans take control of Constantinople, bringing an end to the East Roman Empire.

ANCIENT HISTORY

KEY DATES

- C. 1000 BCE: Small village communities form in Rome

- 509 BCE: The Roman Republic begins

- 31 BCE: The Roman Empire begins

- 395 CE: The empire is split into West and East

- 476 CE: The West falls

- 1453 CE: The East falls

KEY TOOLS AND TECHNOLOGIES

- The Romans used the arch heavily in architecture, including the Colosseum and the Pantheon. They also invented cement.

- Aqueducts and sewer systems moved clean water and waste. Roman builders perfected multilayer roads that could drain and endure for centuries.

- The Julian calendar Julius Caesar ordered divided months and days into the Roman calendar system, elements of which are in use today.

LANGUAGE

Latin was an official language of the Roman Empire, spoken in the courts and the military, as well as by traders and businessmen. Greek was also a dominant language. Members of the educated upper class studied Greek and were fluent speakers. Inhabitants of conquered lands continued to speak their local languages, but the empire expected these people to learn at least basic Latin.

THE ROMAN ARMY

- Legions: Each legion had approximately 5,000 men, including soldiers, doctors, surveyors, and engineers; they built roads, walls, aqueducts, and tunnels.

- Auxiliaries: Included noncitizens who fought with legionnaires; they were lightly armed and fought as specialized troops, with bows or slings, or as cavalrymen.

- Praetorian Guard: Began with approximately 9,000 men, varied in size over time; remained in the city of Rome and acted as the emperor's bodyguards.

IMPACT OF THE ROMAN CIVILIZATION

- Rome's Republican form of government influenced today's governments.

- The Roman alphabet is still used in English and many other languages.

- Latin is the basis for Italian, French, Spanish, Portuguese, and Romanian.

- Architectural influences can be seen in buildings in many countries around the world, including the US Capitol.

- Christianity, Rome's final official religion, has endured throughout the world.

QUOTE

"In great buildings as well as in other things, the rest of the world has been outdone by us Romans."

—*Pliny the Elder, Roman scholar, 75 CE*

GLOSSARY

aggregate
Crushed rock.

amphitheater
A large oval or circular building with rising tiers of seats, used for watching contests, games, and public events.

augur
A priest who predicted the future.

city-state
A city and its surrounding territory that has its own government.

fresco
A painting made in wet plaster.

frieze
A sculpted or ornamental band on a building.

monarchy
A country ruled by a king or queen.

mosaic
An intricate surface decoration created using small pieces of tile put together to form images.

portent
A natural occurrence that was interpreted as a sign from the gods.

portico
A covered walkway around a building, typically supported by columns.

pumice
A lightweight volcanic glass that has many small holes.

tunic
A garment consisting of two large rectangular pieces of woven cloth—one covering the front, one covering the back—joined at the shoulders.

ADDITIONAL RESOURCES

SELECTED BIBLIOGRAPHY

Barbero, Alessandro. *The Day of the Barbarians: The Battle That Led to the Fall of the Roman Empire*. New York: Walker, 2005. Print.

Bauer, Susan Wise. *The History of the Ancient World: From the Earliest Accounts to the Fall of Rome*. New York: Norton, 2007. Print.

Constable, Nick. *World Atlas of Archeology*. New York: Lyons Press, 2000. Print.

Liberati, Anna Maria, and Fabio Bourbon. *Ancient Rome: History of a Civilization That Ruled the World*. New York: Barnes & Noble, 2006. Print.

FURTHER READINGS

Benoit, Peter. *Ancient Rome*. New York: Scholastic, 2012. Print.

Gimpel, Diane Marczely. *Pompeii*. Minneapolis, MN: Abdo, 2015. Print.

Steele, Philip. *Navigators: Ancient Rome*. New York: Kingfisher, 2009. Print.

WEBSITES

To learn more about Ancient Civilizations, visit **booklinks.abdopublishing.com**. These links are routinely monitored and updated to provide the most current information available.

PLACES TO VISIT

FLAVIAN AMPHITHEATRE (COLOSSEUM)

Piazza del Colosseo, 1 Rome, RM, Lazio, 00184, Italy

+39-06-39967700

http://archeoroma.beniculturali.it/en/archaeological-site/colosseum

The world's largest amphitheater is in the heart of Rome and offers guided and audio tours.

ROMAN PANTHEON

Piazza della Rontonda, Rome, Italy

+39-06-68300230

http://www.rome.info/pantheon

The Pantheon is the best-preserved and most influential building of ancient Rome.

RUINS OF POMPEII

Pompeii, Italy

+39-081 8575111

http://www.pompeiisites.org

Explore the excavation site of the city of Pompeii, which the Vesuvius eruption destroyed and preserved, capturing an example of life from the first century CE.

SOURCE NOTES

Chapter 1. A Mighty Empire

1. "Julius Caesar." *History*. AETN UK, 2014. Web. 23 Sept. 2014.

2. Garrett G. Fagan. "Augustus (31 B.C.–14 A.D.)." *De Imperatoribus Romanis*. Garrett G. Fagan, 5 July 1994. Web.

3. Amy Chua. *Day of Empire: How Hyperpowers Rise to Global Dominance—and Why They Fall*. New York: Anchor, 2007. XXII. *Google Book Search*. Web. 23 Sept. 2014.

4. Mary T. Boatwright. *Peoples of the Roman World*. New York: Cambridge UP, 2007. 96. *Google Book Search*. Web. 23 Sept. 2014.

Chapter 2. Humble Beginnings

1. A. M. Eckstein. "Hannibal." *World Book Advanced*. World Book, 2014. Web. 27 July 2014.

2. Susan Wise Bauer. *The History of the Ancient World: From the Earliest Accounts to the Fall of Rome*. New York: Norton, 2007. Print. 663.

3. Yaron Z. Eliav. "Jews and Judaism 70–429 CE." *A Companion to the Roman Empire*. David S. Potter, ed. New York: Wiley, 2009. 565. *Google Book Search*. Web. 23 Sept. 2014.

4. "24 August—Mt. Vesuvius Erupts." *History*. AETN UK, 2014. Web. 23 Sept. 2014.

Chapter 3. The Government and Economy

1. William Smith, ed. *Dictionary of Greek and Roman Antiquities.* London, UK: Walton and Maberly, 1853. 1017. *Google Book Search.* Web. 24 Sept. 2014.

2. Tony Allen. *Life, Myth, and Art in Ancient Rome.* Los Angeles, CA: Getty, 2005. 72. *Google Book Search.* Web. 23 Sept. 2014.

Chapter 4. Daily Life

1. Anna Maria Liberati. *Ancient Rome: History of a Civilization that Ruled the World.* New York: Barnes & Noble, 2004. Print. 61.

2. Carol King. "The Romans: What They Wore." *Italy Magazine.* Italy Magazine, 14 Apr. 2014. Web. 23 Sept. 2014.

3. "Theater of Marcellus." *A View on Cities.* www.aviewoncities.com, 2014. Web. 23 July 2014.

4. Keith Hopkins. "The Colosseum: Emblem of Rome." *BBC.* BBC. 22 Mar. 2011. Web. 23 Sept. 2014.

5. Mark Cartwright. "Circus Maximus." *Ancient History Encyclopedia.* Ancient History Encyclopedia Limited, 12 June 2013. Web. 23 Sept. 2014.

6. Mike Dash. "Blue Versus Green: Rocking the Byzantine Empire." *Smithsonian.* Smithsonian Institution, 2 Mar. 2012. Web. 23 Sept. 2014.

SOURCE NOTES CONTINUED

Chapter 5. Architecture and Art

1. Paul Halsall. "Ancient History Sourcebook: Pliny the Elder (23/4-79 CE): The Grandeur of Rome, c. 75 CE from Natural History." *Fordham University*. Fordham University, June 1998. Web. 23 Sept. 2014.

2. "Colosseum." *History*. A&E Television Networks, 2014. Web. 23 Sept. 2014.

3. Ibid.

4. "Amphitheatres | Roman Amphitheatre List." *Historvius*. LilyPad, n.d. Web. 23 Sept. 2014.

5. "Pantheon." *Lonely Planet*. Lonely Planet, 2014. Web. 24 Sept. 2014.

6. Nick Squires. "Rome's Pantheon May Have Been Built as a Massive Sundial Researchers Reveal." *Telegraph*. Telegraph Media, 1 Aug. 2014. Web. 23 Sept. 2014.

7. "Capitoline Museums." *Buffalo Architecture and History*. Chuck LaChiusa, 2013. Web. 23 Sept. 2014.

8. "Roman Painting." *Metropolitan Museum of Art*. Metropolitan Museum of Art, 2014. Web. 23 Sept. 2014.

Chapter 6. Gods and Goddesses

1. "Vestal Virgins." *Encyclopædia Britannica*. Encyclopædia Britannica, 2014. Web. 24 Sept. 2014.

Chapter 7. Builders and Craftsmen

1. Gregory S. Aldrete. *Daily Life in the Roman City: Rome, Pompeii, and Ostia*. Westport, CT: Greenwood, 2004. 22. *Google Book Search*, 2014. Web. 23 Sept. 2014.

2. William Harris. "How Tunnels Work." *How Stuff Works*. HowStuffWorks, 2014. Web. 23 Sept. 2014.

3. Roger D. Hansen. "Water and Wastewater Systems in Imperial Rome." *WaterHistory.org*. Water History, n.d. Web. 23 Sept. 2014.

4. Arthur M. Eckstein. "Appian Way." *World Book Advanced*. World Book, 2014. Web. 3 June 2014.

5. "Rome, Ancient: Road Construction." *Encyclopædia Britannica*. Encyclopædia Britannica, 2014. Web. 23 Sept. 2014.

Chapter 8. Might of the Legions

1. Barbara F. McManus. "The Roman Army, Part II." *VROMA.org*. VROMA, 1999. Web. 23 Sept. 2014.

2. Richard Alston. *Soldier and Society in Roman Egypt: A Social History*. New York: Routledge, 1995. 31–32. *Google Book Search*. Web. 23 Sept. 2014.

3. Andrew Lintott. *The Romans in the Age of Augustus*. New York, Wiley, 2010. 161. *Google Book Search*. Web. 23 Sept. 2014.

4. Matthew Bunson. *A Dictionary of the Roman Empire*. New York: Oxford UP, 1991. 342. *Google Book Search*. Web. 23 Sept. 2014.

5. Mark Cartwright. "Trajan's Column." *Ancient History Encyclopedia*. Ancient History Encyclopedia Limited, 8 June 2013. Web. 23 Sept. 2014.

6. Ibid.

7. Ibid.

Chapter 9. The Legacy of Rome

1. Jed W. Atkins. *Cicero on Politics and the Limits of Reason: The Republic and Laws*. Cambridge, UK: Cambridge UP, 2013. 1. *Cambridge University Press*. Cambridge University Press, 2014. Web. 23 Sept. 2014.

2. Ibid.

3. L. M. Roth. "St. Paul's Cathedral." *World Book Advanced*. World Book, 2014. Web. 23 Sept. 2014.

4. L. M. Roth. "Arc de Triomphe." *World Book Advanced*. World Book, 2014. Web. 23 Sept. 2014.

INDEX

ABOUT THE AUTHOR

Susan E. Hamen has written numerous children's books on various topics, including the Wright brothers, Pearl Harbor, World War II, the Industrial Revolution, and engineering. Her book *Clara Barton: Civil War Hero and American Red Cross Founder* made the American Library Association's 2011 Amelia Bloomer Book List. Hamen lives in Minnesota with her husband and two children. Her favorite activities include traveling with her family, reading with her kids, and spending time around the campfire on chilly autumn nights.

ABOUT THE CONSULTANT

Thomas Keith has a PhD in classical studies from the University of Chicago. He is an adjunct instructor in the Department of Classics at Loyola University Chicago, specializing in the literature and culture of classical antiquity (Greece and Rome).